MANIFEST
YOUR DESTINY

A holistic approach to creating your best life.

NJ Lewis

CONTENTS

Welcome and Overview	1
The Power of Positive Thinking	3
Understanding Manifestation	5
Setting Clear Intentions	16
Overcoming Manifestation Blocks	26
Creating an Empowering Environment	38
Aligning Actions with Intentions	52
Pioneering people and Law of attraction techniques	61

WELCOME AND OVERVIEW

Manifestation is a compelling concept rooted in the idea that our thoughts, beliefs, and energies can shape our reality. At its core, manifestation is the process of bringing into existence the experiences, opportunities, and outcomes we desire in our lives through intentional thought and focused energy.

Central to the concept is the belief in the law of attraction, which posits that like attracts like. In other words, the energy we emit into the universe through our thoughts and feelings is mirrored to us in the form of circumstances, events, and relationships. This dynamic interplay between our internal state and external reality underscores our mindset's profound influence on the unfolding of our lives.

The key to manifestation lies in setting clear and positive intentions. This involves articulating precisely what we want to attract into our lives and aligning our thoughts and emotions with those desires. Intentions are the guiding force, directing our focus and energy toward a specific goal or outcome. Visualisation, a powerful manifestation tool, complements this process by encouraging individuals to vividly imagine and feel the reality they wish to create.

However, manifestation is not merely wishful thinking. It requires a deeper understanding of one's beliefs and the identification of any limiting thoughts that may act as obstacles. By recognising and reshaping these limiting beliefs, individuals can create a more fertile ground for the seeds of positive intentions to take root and flourish.

Manifestation is not about instant gratification but rather a journey of personal transformation. It involves cultivating patience, trust, and a deep sense of self-awareness. As individuals embark on this journey, they learn to navigate the ebb and flow of life with intention and mindfulness, recognising that their internal state is intricately connected to the external world.

Ultimately, manifestation invites us to become conscious co-creators of our reality, inviting positive change by harnessing the extraordinary power within our thoughts and emotions. It's a profound exploration of the relationship between mind and matter, offering the potential for a more intentional, purposeful, and fulfilling life.

THE POWER OF POSITIVE THINKING

The transformative power of positive thinking in manifestation lies at the heart of this dynamic process, influencing the very fabric of our reality through the energy we project into the universe. Positive thinking is not merely an optimistic outlook; it is a potent force that shapes the course of our lives by drawing in corresponding energies and experiences.

Shaping Beliefs and Perceptions:

Positive thinking serves as a catalyst for reshaping beliefs and perceptions. When individuals cultivate a positive mindset, they shift away from limiting beliefs that may hinder their progress. This transformation allows for a more expansive and empowering view of what is possible.

Attracting Positive Energy:

Like attracts like, and positive thoughts emit a vibrational frequency that resonates with positive energy in the universe. This alignment attracts circumstances, opportunities, and individuals with similar positive vibrations, creating a harmonious and uplifting environment.

Enhancing Resilience:

Positive thinking fosters resilience in the face of challenges. Rather than succumbing to negativity, individuals with an optimistic mindset view obstacles as opportunities for growth. This resilience contributes to a more buoyant and adaptable approach to life's fluctuations.

Empowering Emotional Well-Being:

Positive thinking has a direct impact on emotional well-being. Optimistic thoughts generate positive emotions, such as joy, gratitude, and hope. These emotions, in turn, create a conducive internal environment for manifestation by elevating one's overall emotional state.

Clarifying Intentions:

Positive thinking brings clarity to intentions. When individuals focus on what they want rather than what they lack, they articulate their desires with precision and conviction. This clarity is essential for effective manifestation, guiding the universe in delivering aligned experiences.

Cultivating a Magnet for Success:

Positive thinking transforms individuals into magnets for success. By radiating confidence and a belief in possibilities, they naturally draw in opportunities and resources that align with their positive mindset. This magnetism amplifies their ability to manifest their aspirations.

Fostering a Healthy Mind-Body Connection:

The mind and body are interconnected, and positive thinking improves overall health. Optimistic thoughts have been linked to reduced stress, improved immune function, and enhanced well-being, creating a holistic foundation for successful manifestation.

Inspiring Action and Initiative:

Positive thinking inspires proactive and intentional action. Individuals with a positive mindset are more likely to take the steps necessary to manifest their goals, as they believe in their capacity to influence outcomes through their thoughts and actions.

In essence, the transformative power of positive thinking in manifestation is a profound recognition of the interconnectedness between our internal state and the unfolding of our external reality. By consciously choosing positive thoughts and fostering an optimistic mindset, individuals become active participants in co-creating a reality that aligns with their deepest desires and aspirations.

1

UNDERSTANDING MANIFESTATION

WHAT IS MANIFESTATION?

Manifestation is the process of bringing into reality specific desires, goals, or outcomes through intentional thought, belief, and focused energy. It operates on the principle that our thoughts and emotions can influence the external world, shaping our experiences and circumstances. The core concept of manifestation is often associated with the law of attraction, which suggests that like attracts like—the energy you emit into the universe attracts similar energies or events back to you.

Key Components of Manifestation:

Intention Setting:

Manifestation begins with setting clear and specific intentions. This involves identifying what you want to manifest, whether a specific goal, a change in circumstances, or an emotional state.

Positive Thinking and Belief:

Positive thinking plays a crucial role in manifestation. Maintaining an optimistic mindset helps align your energy with your intentions. Believing in the possibility of achieving your goals enhances the effectiveness of the manifestation process.

Visualisation:

Visualisation is a powerful tool in manifestation. It involves creating mental images of your desired outcomes as if they have already occurred. You reinforce a positive and focused mindset by vividly imagining the details, emotions, and experiences associated with your goals.

Emotional Alignment:

Emotions are a significant driving force in manifestation. Aligning your emotions with the positive outcomes you seek strengthens the vibrational energy you emit. Cultivating feelings of joy, gratitude, and confidence enhances the manifestation process.

Mindfulness and Awareness:

Being mindful of your thoughts and staying aware of the present moment is essential in manifestation. Mindfulness helps you identify and shift any negative or limiting beliefs that might hinder the manifestation of your desires.

Taking Aligned Action:

Manifestation involves more than just positive thinking; it requires taking intentional and aligned action toward your goals. Action serves as a bridge between your intentions and the physical manifestation of your desires.

HOW MANIFESTATION WORKS:

Energy and Vibration:

Everything in the universe is energy, and each thought and emotion carries a particular vibrational frequency. Manifestation works by aligning your energy with the frequencies of the outcomes you desire, attracting similar energies from the external environment.

Subconscious Mind Influence:

The subconscious mind, which holds deep-seated beliefs and patterns, is essential in manifestation. Reprogramming limiting beliefs and fostering a positive subconscious mindset enhances the alignment between your thoughts and your external reality.

Resonance with the Universe:

The universe is considered to be responsive to our energetic vibrations. When your thoughts, emotions, and actions resonate with the frequencies of your intentions, it is believed that the universe responds by bringing circumstances and opportunities into your life that align with those intentions.

Law of Attraction:

The law of attraction posits that focusing on positive or negative thoughts can bring positive or negative experiences into one's life. By consciously directing your thoughts and energy toward what you want, you are said to attract similar experiences or energies.

In essence, manifestation is a dynamic interplay between thoughts, beliefs, emotions, and actions that shapes the reality you experience. It's a holistic approach involving internal alignment and intentional engagement with the external world, emphasising the interconnectedness between the mind and the unfolding of life's experiences.

THE LAW OF ATTRACTION AND THE ROLE OF THOUGHTS AND BELIEFS

The law of attraction is a foundational principle in the field of manifestation, suggesting that like attracts like. This universal law asserts that the energy you emit into the universe, primarily through your thoughts and beliefs, attracts similar energies or experiences back to you. The law of attraction operates on the premise that your predominant thoughts, emotions, and beliefs shape your reality, influencing the circumstances and events that manifest in your life.

Key Components of the Law of Attraction:

Thoughts as Energy:

According to the law of attraction, thoughts are not merely fleeting ideas but energy with a vibrational frequency. Positive thoughts emit positive energy, and negative thoughts emit negative energy. The quality of your thoughts determines the quality of the energy you send out into the universe.

Emotions and the Power of Feelings:

Emotions are powerful amplifiers in the manifestation process. The law of attraction emphasises the importance of aligning your emotions with your desires. When you feel joy, gratitude, and confidence, you generate a positive vibrational frequency that attracts similar positive experiences.

Beliefs as Magnetic Forces:

Beliefs act as magnetic forces that draw corresponding experiences into your life. If you hold limiting beliefs or doubts about your ability to achieve a goal, the law of attraction suggests that these beliefs can repel the outcomes you desire. Aligning your beliefs with your intentions strengthens the attraction process.

Focused Attention:

The law of attraction responds to your focused attention to particular thoughts. By consistently directing your thoughts toward what you want to manifest, you intensify the energetic signal you send to the universe. This focused attention helps create a resonance between your internal state and external circumstances.

THE ROLE OF THOUGHTS AND BELIEFS:

Positive vs. Negative Thoughts:

Positive thoughts are believed to attract positive experiences, while negative thoughts can draw negative circumstances. The law of attraction encourages individuals to shift their thinking patterns from focusing on what they lack to what they want to create.

Conscious and Subconscious Mind Influence:

Both conscious and subconscious thoughts play a role in the law of attraction. While conscious thoughts are those you are aware of, subconscious thoughts are deeply ingrained beliefs that may operate beneath your conscious awareness. Reprogramming limiting beliefs in the subconscious mind is crucial for effective manifestation.

Affirmations and Visualisation:

Affirmations and visualisation leverage the power of thoughts in the manifestation process. Affirmations involve repeating positive statements to reinforce desired beliefs, while visualisation entails creating mental images of your goals as if they have already been achieved.

Consistency and Persistence:

The law of attraction emphasises the importance of consistent and persistent positive thinking. It's not just about occasional bursts of positivity but maintaining an ongoing, optimistic mindset. Consistency amplifies the vibrational signal you emit.

Alignment with Desires:

Thoughts and beliefs need to align with your desires for the law of attraction to work effectively. A conflict between what you consciously want and your underlying beliefs can create resistance and hinder the manifestation process.

In summary, the Law of Attraction underscores the influential role of thoughts and beliefs in shaping our experiences. By consciously directing our thoughts toward positive outcomes, aligning our beliefs with our goals, and fostering a positive emotional state, we actively participate in the co-creation of our reality. The law of attraction invites individuals to be mindful of the energy they emit into the universe and to harness the transformative power of their thoughts and beliefs for positive manifestation.

THE IMPACT OF POSITIVE THINKING ON ONE'S MINDSET.

Positive thinking profoundly impacts one's mindset, influencing how individuals perceive themselves, their experiences, and the world around them. The power of positive thinking extends beyond momentary optimism; it shapes the overall mindset, fostering resilience, enhancing well-being, and influencing the trajectory of one's life. Here are key aspects of the impact of positive thinking on mindset:

Shift in Perspective:

Positive thinking initiates a shift in perspective. Instead of dwelling on challenges or setbacks, individuals with a positive mindset are inclined to view difficulties as opportunities for growth. This change in perspective contributes to a more optimistic and solution-oriented approach to life.

Enhanced Resilience:

Positive thinking is closely linked to resilience—the ability to bounce back from adversity. When faced with challenges, individuals who maintain a positive mindset are more likely to persevere, learn from setbacks, and adapt to changing circumstances. The resilience cultivated through positive thinking strengthens mental fortitude.

Optimism and Hope:

Positive thinking instills optimism and hope. It cultivates a belief that favorable outcomes are possible, even in challenging situations. This optimistic outlook serves as a motivating force, inspiring individuals to pursue their goals with enthusiasm and determination.

Reduction of Stress and Anxiety:

Positive thinking contributes to a reduction in stress and anxiety. Individuals mitigate the impact of stressors by focusing on the positive aspects of a situation. The ability to approach challenges with a calm and positive mindset supports mental and emotional well-being.

Increased Self-Efficacy:

Positive thinking is linked to increased self-efficacy—the belief in one's ability to achieve goals. Individuals with a positive mindset are more likely to set ambitious but attainable goals and be confident in their capacity to overcome obstacles and succeed.

Improved Emotional Well-Being:

Positive thinking is associated with improved emotional well-being. Individuals create a more uplifting internal environment by cultivating positive thoughts and emotions. This positivity extends to relationships, enhancing social connections and overall life satisfaction.

Enhanced Problem-Solving Skills:

A positive mindset enhances problem-solving skills. Individuals approach challenges creatively and constructively, exploring solutions rather than getting bogged down by the problems. Positive thinking encourages flexibility and adaptability in finding effective solutions.

Physical Health Benefits:

Positive thinking has been linked to physical health benefits. The reduction of stress, promotion of healthier behaviours, and the overall positive impact on the mind-body connection contribute to a healthier lifestyle. This, in turn, can have positive effects on physical health.

Social and Interpersonal Benefits:

Positive thinking influences social interactions and relationships. Individuals with a positive mindset are generally more approachable, supportive, and empathetic. This positivity fosters harmonious connections with others, contributing to a positive social environment.

Cultivation of Gratitude:

Positive thinking often involves the cultivation of gratitude. Appreciating the positive aspects of life, both big and small, encourages a mindset of abundance. Gratitude reinforces positive thinking by acknowledging and valuing the good in one's life.

In essence, positive thinking influences a transformative shift in mindset. It empowers individuals to navigate life with resilience, optimism, and a proactive approach. By fostering a positive mindset, individuals not only enhance their mental and emotional well-being but also create a foundation for personal growth, success, and a more fulfilling life.

THE CONNECTION BETWEEN THOUGHTS, EMOTIONS, AND OUTCOMES

The connection between thoughts, emotions, and outcomes is a fundamental aspect of human experience, shaping how individuals perceive and interact with the world. This interconnected relationship underscores the impact of mental and emotional states on the outcomes and experiences individuals manifest in their lives. Here's an exploration of this intricate connection:

Thoughts as Precursors to Emotions:

Thoughts serve as the initial catalyst in this connection. The way individuals interpret events, situations, or stimuli shapes their thoughts. These thoughts, positive or negative, influence the subsequent emotional response.

Emotions as Energy in Motion:

Emotions are the energetic responses to thoughts. They reflect the interpretation and meaning individuals assign to their thoughts. Emotions can range from joy and gratitude to fear and frustration, and they carry a powerful vibrational energy that permeates one's internal and external environment.

Impact of Emotions on Perception:

Emotions colour the lens through which individuals perceive the world. Positive emotions tend to broaden awareness, enhance creativity, and foster a sense of well-being. Conversely, negative emotions can narrow focus, trigger stress responses, and contribute to a more limited perspective.

Feedback Loop Between Thoughts and Emotions:

There exists a continuous feedback loop between thoughts and emotions. Thoughts can trigger emotions, and in turn, emotions can reinforce or modify thoughts. This dynamic interplay can either perpetuate a cycle of positivity or negativity, depending on the nature of thoughts and emotions.

Influence on Decision-Making:

Thoughts and emotions play a pivotal role in decision-making. The emotional charge associated with a particular thought can significantly impact individuals' choices. Decisions influenced by positive emotions often lead to more favourable outcomes, while decisions influenced by negative emotions may have less favourable consequences.

Vibrational Alignment with Outcomes:

Thoughts and emotions emit vibrational frequencies that resonate with similar frequencies in the external environment. The law of attraction posits that individuals attract experiences and outcomes that align with the vibrational energy they emit. Positive thoughts and emotions are believed to attract positive outcomes and vice versa.

Impact on Well-Being:

The nature of thoughts and emotions has a direct impact on overall well-being. Positive thoughts and emotions contribute to a sense of happiness, fulfilment, and overall mental health. Conversely, a pattern of negative thoughts and emotions can contribute to stress, anxiety, and a diminished sense of well-being.

Role in Manifestation and Goal Achievement:

Thoughts and emotions are critical in the manifestation process. When individuals hold positive thoughts and emotions aligned with their goals, they create a fertile ground for the manifestation of desired outcomes. On the contrary, a predominance of negative thoughts and emotions may hinder the realisation of goals.

Adaptation to Resilience:

Positive thoughts and emotions contribute to emotional resilience. When faced with challenges, individuals with a positive mindset are more likely to adapt, learn, and navigate adversity effectively. This resilience enhances the capacity to cope with life's ups and downs.

Mind-Body Connection:

The connection between thoughts, emotions, and outcomes extends to the mind-body connection. Positive thoughts and emotions have been associated with physiological benefits, including lower stress levels, improved immune function, and better overall health.

In summary, the connection between thoughts, emotions, and outcomes is a dynamic and influential aspect of human psychology. Understanding and consciously shaping this connection can empower individuals to cultivate positive mental and emotional states, ultimately influencing the quality of their experiences and the outcomes they manifest in their lives.

SETTING CLEAR INTENTIONS

THE IMPORTANCE OF CLARITY

Clarity is a vital element in the process of manifestation, playing a central role in articulating and achieving one's desires. The importance of clarity in manifestation is evident in various aspects of the practice, influencing the effectiveness of goal setting, visualisation, and the overall manifestation journey. Here's an exploration of why clarity is essential in manifestation:

Precision in Goal Setting:

Clarity brings precision to goal setting. When individuals have a clear and specific vision of what they want to manifest, it becomes easier to articulate their intentions. Vague or ambiguous goals may lead to unclear outcomes, making aligning thoughts and actions with the desired manifestation challenging.

Focused Intention:

Clarity directs focused intention. Knowing exactly what one wishes to manifest allows for a concentrated and purposeful alignment of thoughts and energy. This focused intention is like a magnifying glass that intensifies the vibrational frequency sent to the universe, enhancing the manifestation process.

Elimination of Ambiguity:

Ambiguity in intentions can create confusion in the manifestation process. Clarity eliminates ambiguity, providing a roadmap for the universe to follow in delivering the desired outcomes. It reduces the risk of mixed signals and ensures more straightforward and effective communication with the universe.

Enhanced Visualisation:

Visualisation, a powerful manifestation technique, is strengthened by clarity. The visualisation process becomes more potent when individuals have a vivid and clear mental image of their desired outcomes. Clear visualisation reinforces the emotional and sensory experience associated with the manifestation, creating a more profound impact on the subconscious mind.

Alignment of Beliefs:

Clarity facilitates the alignment of beliefs with intentions. When individuals are clear about their wants, they can better identify and address any conflicting beliefs hindering the manifestation process. This alignment fosters a cohesive and harmonious internal environment for manifestation.

Positive Emotional Engagement:

Clarity evokes positive emotional engagement. Knowing precisely what one is working towards generates a sense of excitement, enthusiasm, and confidence. This positive emotional engagement enhances the overall manifestation experience and produces a more favourable vibrational energy.

Measurable Progress:

Clarity allows for the measurement of progress. Clearly defined goals provide a benchmark for tracking manifestations. Individuals can assess whether their thoughts, actions, and experiences align with their clear intentions, making it easier to adjust strategies if necessary.

Empowerment and Confidence:

Clarity empowers individuals and boosts confidence. A clear vision of what is being manifested instils a sense of purpose and self-assurance. This confidence positively influences the manifestation journey, encouraging perseverance and a belief in the certainty of success.

Effective Communication with the Universe:

The universe is said to respond to clear and intentional communication. Clarity ensures that the universe receives a distinct signal regarding the desired outcomes. It establishes a direct line of communication, making it more likely for the universe to align circumstances and opportunities with the stated intentions.

Quality of Manifested Reality:

Ultimately, the quality of the manifested reality is significantly influenced by clarity. Clear intentions contribute to a more precise and aligned manifestation, increasing the likelihood of experiencing the desired outcomes in a satisfying and fulfilling way.

In summary, the importance of clarity in manifestation cannot be overstated. It acts as a guiding force, enhancing goal setting, visualisation, belief alignment, and overall effectiveness in the manifestation process. Clarity empowers individuals to communicate their desires precisely, fostering a more intentional and purposeful journey toward manifesting their goals.

THE IMPORTANCE OF CLARITY

Clear and specific intentions are paramount in the practice of manifestation, serving as the cornerstone for effectively harnessing the power of the mind and the universe. The need for clear and specific intentions cannot be overemphasised, as they form the basis for focused energy, aligned actions, and successful manifestation. Here's an exploration of why clarity and specificity are crucial in the manifestation process:

Guiding the Mind's Focus:

Clear and specific intentions provide a clear roadmap for the mind. When individuals articulate precisely what they want to manifest, it guides the mind's focus and attention. This focused attention is essential in directing the mind's energy toward the desired outcomes.

Enhancing Visualisation:

Visualisation is a key component of manifestation, and clear intentions enhance this practice. When intentions are specific, individuals can create vivid mental images of their desired reality. This clarity in visualisation strengthens the emotional and sensory experience associated with the manifestation, making it more potent.

Minimising Ambiguity:

Ambiguous intentions create confusion in the manifestation process. Clarity minimises ambiguity, reducing the risk of sending mixed signals to the universe. Ambiguous intentions may lead to unclear outcomes, hindering the manifestation of desires.

Aligning Thoughts and Emotions:

Clear and specific intentions facilitate the alignment of thoughts and emotions. When individuals precisely understand what they want, they can consciously align their thoughts and emotions with those desires. This alignment enhances the vibrational energy emitted into the universe.

Setting Measurable Goals:

Clear intentions make it possible to set measurable goals. Specificity allows individuals to define the parameters of their manifestation, making it easier to track progress. Measurable goals provide a tangible way to assess whether thoughts and actions align with the intended outcomes.

Overcoming Limiting Beliefs:

Specific intentions make it easier to identify and overcome limiting beliefs. When individuals are clear about what they want, they can recognise any conflicting beliefs that might hinder the manifestation process. This awareness empowers them to address and reframe limiting beliefs effectively.

Encouraging Positive Emotional Engagement:

Clear intentions evoke positive emotional engagement. Knowing exactly what one is working towards generates enthusiasm, excitement, and a positive emotional state. Positive emotions contribute to a more favourable vibrational energy, aligning with the principles of successful manifestation.

Facilitating Effective Communication with the Universe:

The universe is believed to respond to clear and intentional communication. Clear intentions serve as a direct and specific message to the universe, enhancing the likelihood of receiving aligned circumstances and opportunities. This effective communication is crucial in the manifestation process.

Increasing the Power of Affirmations:

Affirmations, which are positive statements reinforcing intentions, are more powerful when intentions are clear and specific. Precision in affirmations enhances their impact on the subconscious mind, aligning it with the intended outcomes.

Creating a Detailed Vision:

Clear intentions contribute to the creation of a detailed vision of the desired reality. This vision serves as a mental blueprint that individuals can refer to and reinforce regularly. A detailed vision enriches the manifestation process, making the experience more immersive and impactful.

In essence, the need for clear and specific intentions in manifestation is foundational to the entire process. It guides the mind, enhances visualisation, minimises ambiguity, aligns thoughts and emotions, and fosters effective communication with the universe. By articulating intentions with clarity, individuals set the stage for a purposeful and intentional journey toward realising their desires.

SETTING CLEAR AND SPECIFIC INTENTIONS

Well-crafted intentions in manifestation are clear, specific, positive, and aligned with the individual's goals and desires. These intentions should be stated in the present tense as if they are already happening, creating a sense of immediacy and conviction. Here are examples of well-crafted intentions in various areas of life:

Career and Professional Development:

"I am thriving in a fulfilling career that allows me to express my creativity and make a meaningful impact on others."

Abundance and Prosperity:

"I am grateful for the abundant opportunities and financial prosperity flowing into my life effortlessly and consistently."

Health and Well-Being:

"I am in vibrant health, full of energy, and my body is thriving with every passing day."

Relationships and Love:

"I am attracting and nurturing loving, supportive relationships that bring joy and fulfilment into my life."

Personal Growth and Self-Improvement:

"I am continuously growing and evolving into the best version of myself, embracing new opportunities for learning and personal development."

Happiness and Positivity:

"I am radiating positivity and happiness, attracting uplifting experiences and people into my daily life."

Spiritual Connection:

"I am deepening my spiritual connection, gaining insight, and experiencing inner peace and serenity."

Creativity and Expression:

"I am tapping into my creative potential, expressing myself authentically, and contributing unique value to the world."

Travel and Adventure:

"I am exploring new and exciting destinations, immersing myself in diverse cultures, and creating unforgettable travel experiences."

Mindfulness and Inner Peace:

"I am cultivating mindfulness in every moment, finding inner peace, and approaching challenges with calm and centeredness."

Remember, the key is to be specific and clear about what you want, ensuring that your intentions resonate with your true desires. Additionally, infusing your intentions with positive emotions and a sense of gratitude is beneficial, as this enhances the vibrational energy you are sending out into the universe. Regularly affirming and visualising these intentions can further amplify their impact on your subconscious mind and the manifestation process.

VISUALISATION AS A POWERFUL MANIFESTATION TOOL

Visualisation is a powerful tool in manifestation, leveraging the mind's ability to create detailed mental images and scenarios to influence the subconscious mind, emotions, and overall energy. Here's an explanation of how visualisation contributes to the manifestation process:

VISUALISATION EXERCISE

Practical visualisation exercises are effective for manifesting goals and desires. Here's a short step-by-step guide to help you engage in a practical visualisation exercise:

Step 1: Set Clear Intentions:

Begin by clearly defining what you want to manifest. Be specific about your goals and desires. The clearer your intentions, the more focused and effective your visualisation will be.

Step 2: Find a Quiet Space:

Choose a quiet and comfortable space where you won't be disturbed. This could be a room, a quiet corner, or a peaceful outdoor setting.

Step 3: Get in a Comfortable Position:

Sit or lie down in a comfortable position. Ensure that your body is relaxed and there's no muscle tension. Close your eyes to eliminate external distractions.

Step 4: Deep Breathing for Relaxation:

Take a few deep breaths to relax your body and calm your mind. Inhale deeply through your nose, hold for a moment, and exhale slowly through your mouth. Repeat this several times until you feel a sense of relaxation.

Step 5: Visualise with Detail:

Begin to visualise your desired outcome. Picture it in your mind as if it's happening right now. Include vivid details such as colours, shapes, and relevant sensory experiences. Imagine the scenario with as much clarity as possible.

Step 6: Engage Your Senses:

Bring your senses into the visualisation. Feel the textures, hear the sounds, and even imagine any scents or tastes associated with your desired outcome. The more senses you engage, the more immersive and powerful the visualisation becomes.

Step 7: Emotional Connection:

Allow yourself to feel the emotions associated with successfully manifesting your goal. Let these emotions flow through you, whether joy, gratitude, or a sense of accomplishment. Emotion is a key element in the manifestation process.

Step 8: Positive Affirmations:

While visualising, incorporate positive affirmations related to your goal. Affirmations reinforce the belief that your desired outcome is not only possible but is already in the process of manifesting.

Step 9: Express Gratitude:

Conclude your visualisation by expressing gratitude for the manifestation of your goals. Feel thankful for the success and abundance that you've visualised.

Step 10: Open Your Eyes Slowly:

When you're ready, open your eyes slowly. Take a moment to transition back to your surroundings. Carry the positive energy and belief from your visualisation into your daily life.

Repeat the visualisation regularly. Consistency is key in reinforcing the desired outcomes in your subconscious mind. The more you practice, the more ingrained the images and emotions become.

3

OVERCOMING MANIFESTATION BLOCKS

Be open to opportunities and take inspired action in alignment with your goals. Visualisation is a powerful precursor to action, and by taking intentional steps, you contribute to the manifestation process.

Remember, the key to effective visualisation is consistency, clarity of intentions, and emotional engagement. Regularly practising practical visualisation exercises aligns your mind, emotions, and energy with your goals, fostering a positive and proactive mindset for successful manifestation.

LIMITING BELIEFS

Limiting beliefs are deeply ingrained convictions or thought patterns that can hinder personal growth and success. In the context of manifestation, these beliefs can act as barriers, preventing individuals from realising their goals and desires. Identifying and addressing limiting beliefs is a crucial step in the manifestation process. Here are some common limiting beliefs and how they may impact manifestation:

"I'm Not Worthy":

This belief centres around a lack of self-worth and can sabotage efforts to manifest positive outcomes. If deep down you feel undeserving of success or abundance, it can create a subconscious resistance to manifesting those very things.

"I Don't Deserve Happiness":

Similar to the unworthiness belief, feeling undeserving of happiness can block the manifestation of joyful experiences. This belief may arise from past experiences, societal conditioning, or negative self-perception.

"Success Is Not Meant for Me":

Believing that success is reserved for others but not oneself can limit the ability to manifest achievements. This belief often stems from comparisons, societal expectations, or past failures.

"I'll Never Have Enough Money":

Financial abundance is a common desire in manifestation, but a belief in perpetual lack can counteract efforts to attract prosperity. This belief may result from past financial struggles or a scarcity mindset.

"Fear of Failure":

The fear of failure can be a significant barrier. If you believe that failure is inevitable or that it defines your worth, it can hinder your willingness to take risks and pursue ambitious goals.

"I'm Not Talented Enough":

Believing in a lack of skills or talent can impede the pursuit of passions and goals. This belief may stem from comparisons with others or past experiences of perceived inadequacy.

"I Can't Change":

This limiting belief suggests a resistance to personal growth and change. If you believe that change is impossible, it can obstruct the manifestation of a better and more fulfilling life.

"I'm Too Old/Young":

Age-related beliefs can limit possibilities. Feeling too old or too young to achieve certain goals can create mental barriers that hinder manifestation efforts.

"It's Selfish to Prioritise Myself":

Believing that prioritising personal desires is selfish can hinder the manifestation of self-improvement and personal goals. This belief often comes from societal expectations and a misplaced sense of responsibility.

"I Must Always Put Others First":

Similar to the previous belief, constantly putting others first can hinder self-manifestation. While helping others is admirable, neglecting personal needs and desires can limit individual growth.

Addressing limiting beliefs involves self-awareness, challenging these beliefs, and replacing them with positive and empowering thoughts. Techniques such as affirmations, visualisation, and cognitive-behavioural strategies can effectively reshape limiting beliefs and create a mindset more conducive to successful manifestation. It's important to recognise these beliefs as obstacles and actively work to transform them into empowering and supportive beliefs that align with your goals and desires.

REPROGRAMMING THE SUBCONSCIOUS MIND

Reprogramming the subconscious mind involves intentionally changing deep-seated beliefs, thought patterns, and behaviours stored in the subconscious. The subconscious mind plays a significant role in shaping our habits, reactions, and perceptions, often based on experiences, conditioning, and beliefs formed throughout life. Reprogramming aims to replace negative or limiting aspects with positive, empowering, and supportive beliefs. Here's an overview of the process:

Self-Awareness:

The first step in reprogramming the subconscious mind is awareness of existing beliefs and patterns. This self-awareness involves recognising thought processes, reactions, and behaviours that may be limiting or counterproductive.

Identifying Limiting Beliefs:

Pinpoint specific limiting beliefs that may be holding you back. These beliefs often manifest as negative self-talk or doubts about your abilities, worth, or potential for success.

Challenging Negative Thoughts:

Actively challenge and question negative or limiting thoughts. Ask yourself if these thoughts are based on reality or evidence or simply inherited beliefs that no longer serve you.

Affirmations:

Positive affirmations are concise, positive statements designed to counteract negative beliefs. Repeat affirmations regularly to instil new, positive beliefs into the subconscious. For example, affirmations like "I am worthy of success and happiness" can be powerful if you struggle with self-worth.

Visualisation:

Visualisation involves creating mental images of desired outcomes. By vividly imagining positive scenarios and experiences, you train the subconscious mind to accept new possibilities. Visualisation is effective in reinforcing positive beliefs and expectations.

Hypnosis and Guided Imagery:

Hypnosis and guided imagery involve accessing the subconscious mind in a relaxed state. Practitioners or audio resources guide individuals through visualisations and suggestions, helping reprogram beliefs at a deeper level.

Subliminal Messages:

Subliminal messages are stimuli, often auditory or visual, presented at a level below conscious awareness. While controversial, some believe that subliminal messages can influence the subconscious mind, promoting positive changes.

Neuro-Linguistic Programming (NLP):

NLP is a psychological approach that explores the connections between neurological processes, language, and behavioural patterns. NLP techniques aim to reprogram the way individuals think and respond to situations.

Cognitive-Behavioural Therapy (CBT):

CBT is a therapeutic approach that addresses and modifies negative thought patterns and behaviours. It involves identifying and challenging irrational beliefs and replacing them with more rational and positive ones.

Positive Reinforcement:

Consistently reinforce positive behaviours and thoughts. Celebrate small victories, acknowledge progress, and create an environment that supports the development of new, empowering beliefs.

Consistent Practice:

Reprogramming the subconscious mind is not an instant process. Consistency is crucial. Regularly engage in the chosen techniques, whether affirmations, visualisation, or other methods, to reinforce positive changes over time.

Patience and Persistence:

Changing deep-seated beliefs takes time and persistence. Be patient with yourself and recognise that transformation is a gradual process. Celebrate each step forward, no matter how small.

Reprogramming the subconscious mind is a proactive and intentional process that requires ongoing effort and dedication. By consistently applying these techniques, individuals can gradually replace limiting beliefs with more empowering ones, fostering positive change and personal growth.

THE ROLE OF THE SUBCONSCIOUS MIND IN MANIFESTATION.

The subconscious mind plays an important role in the process of manifestation. While the conscious mind is responsible for logical thinking, reasoning, and decision-making, the subconscious mind operates beneath the surface, influencing emotions, habits, and automatic responses. Understanding the role of the subconscious mind in manifestation is essential for those seeking to intentionally create positive changes in their lives. Here's how the subconscious mind contributes to the manifestation process:

Belief System Storage:

The subconscious mind stores beliefs, attitudes, and perceptions formed throughout life. These positive or negative beliefs shape one's worldview and influence how one interprets and responds to experiences.

Habitual Patterns and Behaviours:

The subconscious mind drives many daily actions and behaviours. Habits, reactions, and automatic responses are often rooted in the programming stored in the subconscious. Manifestation is impacted by these habits, as they shape the consistency of thoughts and actions.

Emotional Responses:

Emotions are closely tied to the subconscious mind. Deep-seated emotional responses to specific situations or concepts are often stored in the subconscious. Depending on their nature, these emotions can either support or hinder the manifestation process.

Memory and Past Experiences:

The subconscious mind holds memories of past experiences, both positive and negative. Past experiences contribute to forming beliefs and expectations about the present and future. Manifestation involves reshaping these memories and associations.

Imagination and Creativity:

The subconscious mind is the seat of imagination and creativity. Visualisation, a powerful manifestation technique, taps into the imaginative capabilities of the subconscious. When vividly imagining desired outcomes, individuals influence the subconscious mind to align with these positive mental images.

Autonomic Functions:

The subconscious mind controls autonomic functions of the body, such as breathing, heartbeat, and digestion. These functions are automatic and operate without conscious control. Maintaining a positive and relaxed state through techniques like deep breathing can positively influence the subconscious mind.

Openness to Suggestions:

The subconscious mind is highly receptive to suggestions, especially when in a relaxed state. This is why practices like affirmations, hypnosis, and guided imagery effectively influence the subconscious. Positive suggestions can replace limiting beliefs and support the manifestation of desired outcomes.

Connection to the Law of Attraction:

The law of attraction suggests that like attracts like. The subconscious mind, driven by beliefs and emotions, emits a vibrational frequency that attracts similar energies from the universe. Positive beliefs and emotions align with the principles of the law of attraction, enhancing the manifestation process.

Influence on Decision-Making:

The subconscious mind often plays a significant role in decision-making, even if individuals believe they are consciously making choices. Manifestation involves aligning subconscious beliefs with conscious intentions, ensuring that decisions support the desired outcomes.

Role in Goal Setting:

The subconscious mind is involved in goal setting and goal achievement. When clear intentions are impressed upon the subconscious through repeated affirmations, visualisation, and positive reinforcement, the mind becomes aligned with the goals, making them more likely to manifest.

Resistance to Change:

The subconscious mind can resist change, especially when it perceives a departure from established beliefs or comfort zones. Overcoming resistance involves gradually reprogramming the subconscious to accept and embrace new, positive beliefs.

Understanding and leveraging the power of the subconscious mind is fundamental to successful manifestation. Techniques that work directly with the subconscious, such as visualisation, affirmations, and other forms of positive reinforcement, help align the mind with desired outcomes and create a positive foundation for manifestation efforts.

EXERCISES AND TECHNIQUES FOR SUBCONSCIOUS REPROGRAMMING.

Reprogramming the subconscious mind involves consistent and intentional practices to replace limiting beliefs with positive and empowering ones. Here are various exercises and techniques to help you reprogram your subconscious mind:

Positive Affirmations:

Create concise, positive statements that reflect the beliefs you want to instil in your subconscious mind. Repeat these affirmations regularly, especially in the morning and before bedtime. For example: "I am worthy of success and abundance."

Visualisation:

Engage in regular visualisation sessions where you vividly imagine achieving your goals. Picture the scenario in great detail, involving all your senses. Visualisation helps align the subconscious mind with positive outcomes.

Vision Board Creation:

Create a vision board by compiling images, quotes, and symbols representing your goals and desires. Place the vision board in a visible location where you can see it daily. This visual representation reinforces positive images in your subconscious.

Subconscious Mind Journaling:

Keep a journal focused on positive aspects of your life. Write about your achievements, strengths, and positive experiences. Regularly reviewing and updating this journal helps shift your focus toward positive aspects, influencing the subconscious mind.

Mindfulness Meditation:

Practice mindfulness meditation to bring awareness to your thoughts and emotions. Mindfulness helps you observe and detach from negative or limiting thoughts, creating space for positive beliefs to take root.

Self-Hypnosis:

Explore self-hypnosis techniques or use guided hypnosis recordings. In a relaxed state, you can introduce positive suggestions to your subconscious mind, such as affirmations or empowering visualisations.

Neuro-Linguistic Programming (NLP):

NLP techniques, such as anchoring and reframing, can effectively reprogram the subconscious. Anchoring involves associating a specific gesture or phrase with a positive state, while reframing helps change the perception of a situation.

Gratitude Practice:

Cultivate a daily gratitude practice. Regularly expressing gratitude helps shift focus from lack to abundance, influencing the subconscious mind to recognise and attract positive experiences.

Mirror Work:

Stand in front of a mirror and recite positive affirmations or compliments to yourself. Direct eye contact enhances the impact of the messages on the subconscious mind.

Energy Psychology Techniques:

Explore energy psychology modalities like Emotional Freedom Techniques (EFT) or tapping. These techniques involve tapping on specific acupressure points while focusing on positive affirmations to release negative energy and reprogram the subconscious.

Creative Visualisation:

Engage in creative visualisation exercises where you mentally rehearse achieving your goals. Imagine the process, the emotions, and the successful outcome in a detailed and positive manner.

Positive Self-Talk:

Monitor your self-talk and replace negative or self-limiting statements with positive affirmations. Be conscious of how you speak to yourself throughout the day.

Autosuggestion:

Repetitively expose yourself to positive suggestions through autosuggestion. Repeatedly affirm positive beliefs, especially during moments of relaxation or before sleep.

Frequency and Repetition:

Reprogramming the subconscious mind requires consistency and repetition. Engage in these exercises daily to reinforce positive messages and beliefs.

Professional Support:

Consider seeking the assistance of a qualified hypnotherapist, therapist, or life coach specialising in subconscious reprogramming. They can guide you through personalised techniques and provide support in your journey.

Remember, the key to successful subconscious reprogramming is consistency, patience, and a genuine belief in the effectiveness of these practices. It's a gradual process, and you'll observe positive shifts in your mindset and behaviour over time.

CREATING AN EMPOWERING ENVIRONMENT

POSITIVE ENERGY IN YOUR SPACE

The environment is pivotal in shaping and influencing various manifestations, ranging from individual behaviours and characteristics to broader societal trends. Manifestation, in this context, refers to the visible outcomes or expressions of underlying factors such as human behaviour, cultural norms, and ecological processes. Here are some ways in which the environment affects manifestation:

Cultural Manifestations:

Language and Communication: The environment, including geographical and historical factors, influences language development. Different cultures may manifest distinct linguistic expressions, affecting communication styles and how ideas are conveyed.

Art and Creativity: Environmental factors, such as landscape, climate, and local traditions, can inspire artistic expression. Artistic manifestations often reflect the unique characteristics of a particular environment.

Social Manifestations:

Norms and Values: The social environment shapes cultural norms and values, influencing how individuals behave and interact within a society. Manifestations of these norms can be observed in everyday social practices and rituals.

Institutions and Systems: The structure of societal institutions, including education, politics, and economics, affects how power and resources are distributed. This, in turn, manifests in social inequalities and power dynamics.

Individual Behaviour:

Psychological Well-being: The physical environment, including access to green spaces, clean air, and natural light, can impact individuals' mental health and well-being. Manifestations of mental health may include stress levels, mood, and cognitive function.

Cultural Influences: Individual behaviours are often shaped by cultural and societal expectations. The manifestation of these influences can be seen in personal choices, lifestyle, and interpersonal relationships.

Environmental Manifestations:

Climate Change and Ecosystems: Human activities impact the environment, leading to manifestations such as climate change, loss of biodiversity, and changes in ecosystems. These environmental changes, in turn, affect human societies and their patterns of living.

Resource Availability: Manifestations of resource scarcity or abundance can influence economic systems, trade patterns, and the overall well-being of communities.

Technological Manifestations:

Innovation and Development: The technological environment affects the pace of innovation and development. Manifestations of technological progress can be observed in various sectors, influencing industries, communication methods, and lifestyle choices.

Global Manifestations:

Globalisation: The interconnectedness of the world through trade, communication, and travel has led to global manifestations of cultural exchange, economic interdependence, and shared challenges.

Understanding how the environment affects manifestation is essential for addressing societal issues, promoting sustainable practices, and fostering positive cultural and individual development. It also highlights the interconnectedness of different aspects of life and the need for holistic approaches to problem-solving.

OFFER TIPS ON CREATING A POSITIVE AND CONDUCIVE SPACE

Creating a positive and conducive space for meditation is essential to enhance your practice and experience deeper states of relaxation and focus. Here are some tips to help you establish a peaceful and uplifting meditation space:

Select a Quiet Location:

Choose a quiet and secluded area where you won't be easily disturbed. This helps minimise external distractions and allows you to focus inward.

Comfortable Seating:

Use a comfortable chair, cushion, or meditation mat to sit on. Ensure your posture is relaxed and supported to avoid physical discomfort during meditation.

Soft Lighting:

Opt for soft, natural light or dim lighting to create a calming atmosphere. Consider using candles, salt lamps, or fairy lights for a gentle and soothing glow.

If possible, integrate natural elements such as plants, flowers, or even a small indoor fountain. Nature-inspired elements can contribute to a sense of tranquillity.

Aromatherapy:

Use calming scents like lavender, chamomile, or eucalyptus to create a pleasant atmosphere. You can use essential oils, incense, or scented candles for aromatherapy.

Minimalistic Design:

Keep the space clutter-free and opt for a minimalistic design. A clean and simple environment helps to clear the mind and promotes a sense of order and peace.

Personal Touch:

Add personal items that hold positive and calming significance for you. This might include meaningful artwork, spiritual symbols, or items that evoke a sense of joy and relaxation.

Quiet Background Music or Sounds:

Play soft, instrumental music or nature sounds in the background if it helps you relax. Ensure that the volume is low so it doesn't become a distraction.

Temperature Control:

Maintain a comfortable room temperature. If possible, regulate the temperature to create an environment that supports relaxation without being too hot or too cold.

Digital Detox:

Turn off electronic devices or put them on silent mode to minimise interruptions. Create a space free from the buzzing of phones or notifications.

Regular Cleaning:

Keep the meditation space clean and well-maintained. Regular cleaning and organisation contribute to a sense of order and tranquillity.

Create a Ritual:

Establish a pre-meditation ritual, such as lighting a candle, taking a few deep breaths, or setting an intention. This signals to your mind that it's time for focused meditation.

Intentional Decor:

Choose decor that promotes serenity, such as soft colours, calming artwork, or symbols that hold personal significance.

Remember that creating a positive meditation space is a personal endeavour, and you can customise it based on your preferences and what brings you a sense of peace and calmness. Experiment with different elements to find what works best for you.

VISION BOARDS AND MANIFESTATION ALTARS:

Vision boards and manifestation altars are tools that people often use to support the manifestation process. While their effectiveness may vary from person to person, many find them beneficial in reinforcing intentions, maintaining focus, and creating a positive mindset. Here's a closer look at the importance of vision boards and manifestation altars in manifestation practices:

Vision Boards:

Visualisation and Clarity:

Vision boards help individuals clarify and visualise their goals and desires. Individuals create a tangible representation of what they want to manifest by compiling images, words, and symbols representing aspirations.

Focus and Intention:

Creating a vision board requires thoughtful selection and arrangement of elements. This process encourages focus and intention, helping individuals stay mindful of their goals and aspirations.

Positive Affirmation:

Vision boards often include positive affirmations and motivational quotes. Regular exposure to these affirmations can contribute to cultivating a positive mindset, reinforcing belief in the possibility of achieving one's desires.

Law of Attraction:

The concept of the law of attraction suggests that focusing on positive thoughts and desires can attract positive experiences into one's life. Vision boards serve as a daily reminder of these positive intentions, aligning with the principles of the law of attraction.

Inspiration and Motivation:

Vision boards can serve as a source of inspiration and motivation. Seeing visual representations of their goals regularly can boost motivation and commitment to taking actions that align with those goals.

Manifestation Altars:

Sacred Space:

Manifestation altars are physical spaces designated for focused intention and manifestation practices. They serve as sacred areas where individuals can connect with their spiritual or inner selves.

Ritual and Routine:

Creating a manifestation altar often involves rituals such as lighting candles, arranging crystals, or incorporating meaningful symbols. Engaging in these rituals establishes a routine that can enhance mindfulness and intention-setting.

Energy Alignment:

Manifestation altars are believed to help align personal energy with the energies of the universe or a higher power. The intentional arrangement of objects and symbols can facilitate a sense of connection and alignment with one's desires.

Mind-Body Connection:

Engaging with a manifestation altar involves the mind-body connection. Through rituals and focused attention, individuals can cultivate a sense of embodiment, reinforcing their commitment to the manifestation process.

Spiritual Connection:

Manifestation altars provide a physical space for those with spiritual beliefs to connect with higher powers or spiritual guides. It becomes a place for prayer, meditation, and reflection.

In summary, vision boards and manifestation altars can be valuable tools in manifestation practices, offering a tangible and symbolic way to set intentions, stay focused, and align personal energy with desired outcomes. Whether used individually or in combination, these tools contribute to a positive and intentional approach to manifesting goals and aspirations.

GUIDE READERS IN CREATING VISION BOARDS AND MANIFESTATION ALTARS.

Creating vision boards and manifestation altars involves a creative and intentional process. Below are detailed instructions for both practices:

VISION BOARD:

Materials Needed:

Poster board or corkboard

Magazines, newspapers, or printed images

Scissors

Glue or tape

Markers, pens, or coloured pencils

Optional: Stickers, inspirational quotes, personal photos

STEPS:

Set Your Intentions:

Begin by reflecting on your goals and intentions. What do you want to manifest in different areas of your life, such as career, relationships, health, and personal development?

Gather Materials:

Collect magazines, newspapers, or printed images that resonate with your goals. Look for pictures, words, and symbols representing the feelings and outcomes you wish to manifest.

Create a Relaxing Environment:

Find a quiet and comfortable space to work on your vision board. Consider playing calming music or lighting a candle to set a positive atmosphere.

Cut and Arrange:

Start cutting out images and words that appeal to you. Arrange them on the poster board in a way that feels visually pleasing and resonates with your goals. You can create different sections for various aspects of your life.

Add Personal Touch:

Include personal photos, drawings, or handwritten affirmations that hold significance for you. This adds a personal touch and strengthens the emotional connection to your goals.

Glue or Tape:

Once satisfied with the arrangement, glue or tape the images onto the board. Take your time to ensure everything is securely attached.

REFLECT AND DISPLAY:

Sit back and reflect on the completed vision board. Place it in a location where you will see it regularly, such as your bedroom or workspace. Regular visual exposure reinforces your goals.

MANIFESTATION ALTAR:

Materials Needed:

Small table or surface

Cloth or altar cloth

Candles

Crystals or stones

Incense or sage for cleansing

Symbols or objects representing your goals

Personal items with spiritual significance

Optional: Small bowl for offerings, religious or spiritual texts

STEPS:

Select a Sacred Space:

Choose a dedicated and quiet space for your manifestation altar. It could be a small table or any surface that allows you to arrange your items without being disturbed.

Cleanse the Space:

Before setting up your altar, cleanse the space with incense, sage, or any other method you prefer. This helps remove negative energy and creates a sacred atmosphere.

Cover the Surface:

Place a cloth or altar cloth on the table to create a visually appealing and defined space for your altar.

Arrange Crystals and Candles:

Arrange crystals or stones that resonate with your intentions. Place candles around the altar, choosing colours that align with your goals (e.g., white for purity, red for passion).

Symbols of Intentions:

Add symbols or objects representing your goals. For example, if you are manifesting love, include symbols of love or items that evoke feelings of love.

Personal and Spiritual Items:

Include personal items with spiritual significance, such as religious symbols, prayer beads, or items associated with your beliefs.

Light Candles and Incense:

Light the candles and incense. This adds to the ambience and signifies the activation of your altar and the energy associated with your intentions.

Offerings (Optional):

If it aligns with your practice, you can include a small bowl for offerings, such as water, herbs, or grains. This symbolises your commitment and gratitude.

Reflect and Meditate:

Spend time in front of your manifestation altar, reflecting on your intentions. Meditate, pray, or simply focus on the positive energy you've created.

Regular Maintenance:

Keep your manifestation altar clean and organised. Periodically update or rearrange items to align with your evolving goals.

Both vision boards and manifestation altars are personal expressions of your desires and intentions. The key is to infuse them with positive energy, use them as tools for regular reflection, and focus on your goals. Consistent engagement with these practices can help reinforce your commitment to manifesting positive changes in your life.

Taking intentional actions is a pivotal aspect of the manifestation process, as it bridges the gap between setting intentions and realising desired outcomes. While envisioning goals and maintaining a positive mindset are crucial, it is the deliberate and purposeful steps you take that turn aspirations into tangible results. Here's an emphasis on the significance of intentional actions in manifestation:

Transforms Vision into Reality:

Intentional actions are the catalysts that transform your vision into reality. While visualising and affirming your goals are essential, it is through deliberate actions that you bring those aspirations to life.

Aligns Energy and Effort:

Intentional actions align your energy and effort with your desired outcomes. By taking purposeful steps, you direct your focus and resources toward manifesting your goals, creating a powerful synergy between intention and action.

Builds Momentum:

Consistent and intentional actions build momentum. Each step forward creates a sense of progress, motivating and propelling you closer to your objectives. Momentum is a key factor in the manifestation journey.

Demonstrates Commitment:

Action is a tangible expression of your commitment to your goals. It shows that you are dedicated to making your aspirations a reality, reinforcing the belief in your ability to manifest positive changes.

Overcomes Challenges:

Manifestation is not without challenges. Intentional actions empower you to navigate obstacles and setbacks. They provide a proactive approach to problem-solving and resilience in the face of adversity.

Enhances Focus and Clarity:

Engaging in intentional actions enhances focus and clarity. It prompts you to define specific steps and milestones, preventing ambiguity and ensuring a clear path toward the realisation of your goals.

Creates a Feedback Loop:

Action creates a feedback loop that allows you to assess progress and make necessary adjustments. It provides valuable insights into what works, what needs improvement, and how to refine your approach for better results.

Cultivates a Proactive Mindset:

Intentional actions cultivate a proactive mindset. Instead of waiting for circumstances to change, you actively shape your reality through purposeful steps, empowering yourself to take charge of your life.

Attracts Opportunities:

Taking intentional actions opens the door to new opportunities. It positions you in a way that makes you more receptive to opportunities aligned with your goals, creating a dynamic interplay between your efforts and external possibilities.

Enhances Self-Efficacy:

Success in intentional actions enhances your self-efficacy—the belief in your ability to achieve your goals. This increased confidence becomes a powerful force driving further intentional actions and success in manifestation.

In essence, intentional actions serve as the bridge between envisioning a better future and actively creating it. They propel you forward, instil a sense of purpose, and empower you to manifest the positive changes you seek. As you embark on your journey of manifestation, remember that the intentional steps you take today lay the foundation for the reality you'll experience tomorrow.

ALIGNING ACTIONS WITH INTENTIONS

Actions aligned with manifestation goals are intentional, purposeful steps taken to achieve the desired outcomes. These actions vary based on individual goals and intentions, but here are some general examples across different aspects of life:

HEALTH AND WELL-BEING:

Regular Exercise Routine:

Engaging in a consistent exercise routine aligns with manifestation goals related to health and well-being. It can be a deliberate step toward achieving fitness and vitality.

Mindful Eating Habits:

Making intentional choices about what and how you eat contributes to physical well-being. Choosing nourishing foods and practising mindful eating align with health-related manifestation goals.

Prioritising Sleep:

Setting a deliberate sleep schedule and creating a conducive sleep environment align with manifestation goals related to energy, focus, and overall well-being.

CAREER AND PROFESSIONAL DEVELOPMENT:

Setting and Pursuing Career Milestones:

Taking deliberate steps toward achieving career milestones, such as acquiring new skills, pursuing additional education, or actively seeking promotions, aligns with professional manifestation goals.

Networking and Building Relationships:

Actively networking, attending industry events, and building professional relationships are intentional actions that can contribute to career advancement and opportunities.

Creating a Positive Work Environment:

Taking intentional actions to create a positive and productive work environment, such as fostering collaboration or initiating projects, aligns with manifestation goals related to career satisfaction.

RELATIONSHIPS AND PERSONAL GROWTH:

Effective Communication:

Improving communication skills and fostering open, honest communication in relationships aligns with manifestation goals related to building strong and meaningful connections.

Practising Empathy and Compassion:

Cultivating empathy and compassion in interactions with others contributes to positive relationship dynamics and personal growth.

Setting Boundaries:

Intentionally setting and enforcing healthy boundaries in relationships is an action aligned with manifestation goals related to personal well-being and emotional balance.

FINANCIAL ABUNDANCE:

Budgeting and Financial Planning:

Creating a budget, saving money, and engaging in financial planning are intentional actions aligned with manifestation goals related to financial abundance and stability.

Investing in Personal Development:

Allocating resources and time for personal and professional development, such as attending workshops or courses, aligns with manifestation goals related to career growth and financial success.

PERSONAL HAPPINESS AND FULFILLMENT:

Cultivating a Positive Mindset:

Engaging in positive practices, such as gratitude journaling and affirmations, aligns with manifestation goals related to personal happiness and fulfilment.

Pursuing Hobbies and Passions:

Taking intentional steps to engage in hobbies and activities that bring joy and fulfilment aligns with manifestation goals related to personal happiness and a sense of purpose.

Practising Self-Care:

Regular self-care practices, such as meditation, mindfulness, and relaxation, align with manifestation goals related to overall well-being and balance.

Remember, the key is to tailor these actions to your specific goals and intentions. Manifestation is a personal journey, and your actions should resonate with your unique aspirations and vision for a fulfilling life.

CULTIVATING PATIENCE AND TRUST:

Cultivating patience and trust is An important aspect of the manifestation process. While setting intentions and taking intentional actions are essential, the journey toward realising your goals often requires time and a steadfast belief in the process. Here's a detailed exploration of how to cultivate patience and trust in manifestation:

1. Clarify Your Intentions:

Before cultivating patience and trust, it's important to clearly understand your intentions. Define your goals and aspirations with specificity so you have a roadmap for the manifestation journey.

2. Set Realistic Expectations:

Recognise that manifestation is a gradual process. Setting realistic expectations helps you avoid unnecessary frustration and disappointment. Understand that some goals may take time to materialise.

3. Practice Mindfulness and Presence:

Embrace mindfulness and presence in the current moment. Patience is cultivated when you focus on the present instead of constantly anticipating the future. This practice also helps reduce anxiety about the pace of manifestation.

4. Celebrate Small Wins:

Acknowledge and celebrate small victories along the way. Recognising progress, no matter how minor, reinforces your trust in the manifestation process and builds patience by showing that positive changes are happening.

5. Reflect on Past Achievements:

Reflect on instances in your life when things worked out positively, especially when you faced challenges. This reflection can help build trust in your ability to navigate difficulties and manifest desired outcomes.

6. Visualise Success:

Regularly engage in visualisation exercises where you vividly imagine achieving your goals. This practice not only reinforces your intentions but also helps build trust in the power of your thoughts and actions.

7. Affirmations for Patience and Trust:

Create positive affirmations specifically focused on patience and trust in the manifestation process. Repeat these affirmations regularly to reinforce a positive mindset and cultivate these qualities.

8. Embrace Detachment:

Practice detachment from the outcome. While you may have specific goals, allowing flexibility in how they manifest can ease impatience. Trust that the universe may have alternate, sometimes better, paths to fulfil your desires.

9. Journaling:

Maintain a manifestation journal where you record your progress, thoughts, and feelings. This process provides a tangible record of your journey, helping you appreciate the evolution of your goals and reinforcing trust.

10. Seek Support:

Connect with like-minded individuals or mentors who understand the manifestation process. Sharing experiences and receiving support can help you stay patient and reinforce trust during challenging times.

11. Release Negative Thoughts:

Practice letting go of doubts and negative thoughts. Trust that your intentions are valid and that the manifestation process is unfolding in its own time. Releasing negativity creates space for positive energy to flow.

12. Engage in Self-Reflection:

Periodically engage in self-reflection to assess your mindset and beliefs. Identify and challenge any limiting beliefs or impatience hindering the manifestation process.

13. Connect with Gratitude:

Cultivate a sense of gratitude for what you have and the positive changes already happening. Gratitude reinforces a positive mindset and fosters trust in the abundance of the universe.

14. Trust the Timing of Your Life:

Understand that there is a divine timing to the unfolding of your life. Trust that things are happening in alignment with this timing, and what is meant for you will come to fruition at the right moment.

15. Revisit and Refine Goals:

Periodically revisit and refine your goals as needed. This practice allows you to stay connected to your evolving desires and reinforces trust in the adaptability of your manifestation journey.

Cultivating patience and trust is an ongoing process that requires self-awareness, mindfulness, and a positive mindset. By integrating these practices into your daily life, you can navigate the manifestation journey with resilience and a deep-seated belief in the power of your intentions. Remember, the journey is as important as the destination, and patience and trust are valuable companions along the way.

STRATEGIES FOR BUILDING TRUST IN THE UNIVERSE'S TIMING

Building trust in the universe's timing is essential to the manifestation process. It involves cultivating a mindset that acknowledges the inherent wisdom in the unfolding of events and aligns with the belief that everything happens at the right moment. Here are strategies to help you build trust in the universe's timing:

1. Practice Mindfulness:

Description: Engage in mindfulness practices to stay present in the current moment.

How It Builds Trust: Mindfulness helps you appreciate the present and reduces anxiety about the future. By focusing on the now, you develop a deeper understanding of the unfolding journey and the wisdom in each step.

2. Reflect on Past Experiences:

Description: Recall instances when things fell into place at the perfect time in the past.

How It Builds Trust: Reflecting on past experiences reinforces the idea that life has a way of orchestrating events in your favour. Recognise the instances when timing worked out perfectly and use them as anchors for trust.

3. Keep a Gratitude Journal:

Description: Maintain a journal where you express gratitude for the present moment and the progress made.

How It Builds Trust: Gratitude shifts your focus from what's lacking to what's abundant in your life. Regularly acknowledging the positives reinforces trust in the universe's ability to provide and align events for your benefit.

4. Affirmations for Trust:

Description: Create positive affirmations that emphasise trust in divine timing.

How It Builds Trust: Repeating affirmations that reinforce trust rewires your thought patterns. Affirmations serve as constant reminders that the universe's timing is perfect and that everything is unfolding as it should.

5. Visualisation Exercises:

Description: Engage in visualisation exercises where you vividly imagine your goals coming to fruition.

How It Builds Trust: Visualisation creates a mental image of success, fostering a sense of trust in the inevitability of your desired outcomes. Envisioning the manifestation of your goals reinforces your belief in the timing.

6. Develop Patience:

Description: Cultivate patience as a virtue in your daily life.

How It Builds Trust: Patience is closely linked to trust. Embracing patience acknowledges that certain things take time to manifest. By practising patience, you align with the understanding that the universe is working by its timeline.

7. Release Control:

Description: Let go of the need to control every aspect of your life.

How It Builds Trust: Releasing control is an act of surrender and trust. Understand that some things are beyond your control, and trust that the universe has a plan that may exceed your expectations.

8. Connect with Nature:

Description: Spend time in nature, observing its cycles and rhythms.

How it Builds Trust: Nature operates in perfect harmony with its timing. Observing the natural world helps you appreciate the wisdom in cycles and seasons, reinforcing the belief that everything has its own time.

9. Learn from Challenges:

Description: View challenges as opportunities for growth and learning.

How it Builds Trust: Challenges often come with valuable lessons. Trust that even in difficult times, there is a purpose and a lesson to be learned. Each challenge brings you closer to the person you are becoming.

6

PIONEERING PEOPLE AND LAW OF ATTRACTION TECHNIQUES

THE NEVILLE GODDARD LAW OF ATTRACTION TECHNIQUE

Neville Goddard was a prominent figure in the New Thought movement and is known for his teachings on the power of imagination and conscious creation. His manifestation techniques are rooted in the idea that individuals have the ability to shape their reality through their thoughts and beliefs. Here are some key manifestation techniques associated with Neville Goddard:

1. Power of Imagination:

Concept: Neville emphasised the central role of imagination in manifestation. He believed that imagining a desired outcome as if it has already happened is a powerful tool for bringing it into reality.

2. Living in the End:

Concept: Neville taught the concept of living in the end, which means experiencing feelings and emotions as if your desired outcome has already been achieved. By mentally dwelling on the end result, you align your consciousness with the reality you wish to create.

3. Inner Conversations:

Concept: Neville stressed the importance of monitoring and directing your inner conversations. Paying attention to your thoughts and self-talk helps you identify and replace negative or limiting beliefs with positive affirmations aligned with your desires.

4. Feeling is the Secret:

Concept: Neville's book titled "Feeling is the Secret" underscores the significance of emotions in the manifestation process. He taught that it's not just about thinking or imagining; the key is to evoke the emotional experience of having already achieved your goal.

5. Revision Technique:

Concept: Neville introduced the revision technique, where individuals mentally revisit past events and revise them in their imagination to align with desired outcomes. This technique aims to release negative emotional charges associated with past experiences.

6. Pruning Shears of Revision:

Concept: Neville used the metaphor of pruning shears to describe the revision process. Just as you prune a plant to encourage growth, revising your mental images and memories helps shape a more positive and desirable future.

7. Assumption Technique:

Concept: The assumption technique involves assuming the feeling of the wish fulfilled. Neville taught that by embodying the emotions and beliefs associated with your desired outcome, you impress those assumptions upon your subconscious mind.

8. Mental Diets:

Concept: Neville emphasised the importance of maintaining a positive mental diet. This involves consciously choosing thoughts that align with your desires and avoiding thoughts that contradict them. A disciplined mental diet contributes to the manifestation process.

9. Scripting Technique:

Concept: Similar to living in the end, scripting involves writing out a detailed script of your desired reality as if it's happening now. This technique helps to clarify intentions and reinforces the emotional experience of the desired outcome.

It's essential to note that Neville Goddard's teachings are deeply rooted in his interpretation of scripture and metaphysical principles. Individuals interested in applying his manifestation techniques may find it valuable to explore his lectures, books, and recorded teachings for a more comprehensive understanding of his approach. Keep in mind that the interpretation and application of these techniques may vary among practitioners.

DR JOE DISPENZA ON REPROGRAMMING THE MIND

Dr. Joe Dispenza focuses extensively on the idea of reprogramming the mind to create positive and transformative changes in one's life. His teachings draw from neuroscience, quantum physics, and the understanding of consciousness. Here are key elements of Dr. Joe Dispenza's approach to reprogramming the mind:

1. Understanding Neuroplasticity:

Dr. Dispenza emphasises the concept of neuroplasticity, which is the brain's ability to reorganise itself by forming new neural connections throughout life. This concept forms the basis for the idea that the mind can be rewired to create new patterns of thought and behaviour.

2. Breaking the Habit of Being Yourself:

In his book "Breaking the Habit of Being Yourself," Dr. Dispenza explores the neuroscience behind habits and behaviours. He explains how the brain creates and reinforces patterns and how individuals can break free from self-limiting habits by consciously reprogramming the mind.

3. Thoughts and Emotions Influence Biology:

Dr. Dispenza teaches that thoughts and emotions directly impact the body's biology. Negative thoughts and emotions can contribute to stress and illness, while positive thoughts can lead to better health and well-being. Reprogramming the mind involves cultivating positive thoughts and emotions to create a healthier internal environment.

4. Meditation and Mindfulness Practices:

Meditation is a central component of Dr. Dispenza's approach to reprogramming the mind. He guides individuals through meditation practices designed to help them move beyond the analytical mind, access the subconscious, and create a state of coherence between thoughts and feelings.

5. Living in the Present Moment:

Dr. Dispenza encourages individuals to shift their focus from dwelling on the past or worrying about the future to living in the present moment. By being fully present, individuals can consciously choose their thoughts and emotions, contributing to the process of reprogramming.

6. Visualising Desired Outcomes:

Visualisation is a powerful tool in Dr. Dispenza's teachings. He instructs individuals to vividly imagine their desired outcomes, engaging all the senses and emotions associated with success. This process is intended to create a mental blueprint that the brain can work towards manifesting.

7. Changing Beliefs and Assumptions:

Reprogramming the mind involves identifying and changing limiting beliefs and assumptions. Dr. Dispenza encourages individuals to question and challenge old beliefs that no longer serve them, replacing them with empowering beliefs aligned with their goals.

8. Self-Hypnosis Techniques:

Dr. Dispenza incorporates self-hypnosis techniques into his teachings. By entering a state of focused concentration, individuals can bypass the critical mind and directly influence the subconscious, facilitating the process of reprogramming.

9. Quantum Physics and Conscious Creation:

Dr. Dispenza draws from quantum physics to explain the role of consciousness in creating reality. He teaches that through focused intention and elevated emotions, individuals can influence the quantum field and attract positive experiences into their lives.

10. Consistency and Repetition

Reprogramming the mind is a gradual process that requires consistency and repetition. Dr. Dispenza emphasises the importance of daily practices, including meditation and visualisation, to reinforce new patterns of thinking and feeling.

11. Personal Responsibility:

Dr. Dispenza emphasises personal responsibility in the process of reprogramming the mind. Individuals are encouraged to take an active role in their transformation by consciously choosing thoughts, emotions, and actions aligned with their desired outcomes.

12. Neurochemical Changes

Through his work, Dr. Dispenza discusses how reprogramming the mind can lead to neurochemical changes in the brain. Positive thoughts and emotions can release beneficial neurochemicals that contribute to improved well-being and overall health.

13. Community and Support

Dr. Dispenza often highlights the importance of community and support in the process of personal transformation. Connecting with like-minded individuals can provide encouragement, shared experiences, and a supportive environment for reprogramming the mind.

Dr. Joe Dispenza's teachings offer a holistic approach to reprogramming the mind, integrating scientific principles with practical techniques for personal transformation. Individuals interested in applying his methods may explore his books, attend workshops, and engage in meditation practices to gain a deeper understanding and experience of the reprogramming process.

THE SILVA METHOD

The Silva Method is a self-help and personal development program José Silva developed in the 1960s. It is designed to help individuals tap into their inner potential, enhance intuition, and achieve a higher level of mental and emotional well-being. The method incorporates techniques such as meditation, visualisation, and mind-body exercises. Here's an overview of how the Silva Method works:

1. Relaxation Techniques:

The Silva Method begins with relaxation techniques to help individuals achieve a deep physical and mental relaxation state. This is often done through progressive muscle relaxation and breath control to reduce stress and tension.

2. Alpha Brainwave State:

One of the key components of the Silva Method is the focus on reaching the alpha brainwave state. The alpha state is associated with a relaxed and alert mental state, making it easier to access the subconscious mind. Participants are guided to enter this state, where the mind becomes more receptive to positive suggestions and creative visualisation.

3. Visualisation and Mental Imagery:

Visualisation is a central aspect of the Silva Method. Participants are guided to create vivid mental images of their goals and desires. This involves using all the senses to make the visualisation as detailed and immersive as possible. By vividly imagining a desired outcome, individuals can influence their subconscious mind to work towards that goal.

4. Programming Positive Beliefs:

The Silva Method emphasises the power of positive affirmations and beliefs. Participants are encouraged to replace negative or limiting beliefs with positive affirmations. This process is intended to reprogram the subconscious mind to support the individual's goals and aspirations.

5. Mind-Body Healing:

The method incorporates principles of mind-body healing. Participants are guided to use their minds to influence physical well-being, promote relaxation, and even address health issues. The focus is on the interconnectedness of mental and physical states.

6. Intuition Development:

The Silva Method places a strong emphasis on developing and trusting one's intuition. Participants engage in exercises designed to enhance their intuitive abilities. This involves trusting inner guidance and using intuition as a valuable tool in decision-making.

7. Dream Control:

Dream control is another component of the Silva Method. Participants learn techniques to improve dream recall and use their dreams as a source of insight and guidance. Dreams are seen as a reflection of the subconscious mind, and participants are encouraged to harness this resource for personal development.

8. Problem Solving and Goal Setting:

The Silva Method provides tools for problem-solving and goal setting. Participants learn to enter a relaxed state, use creative visualisation to find solutions to challenges, and set clear, achievable goals.

9. Positive Reinforcement and Gratitude:

Participants are encouraged to express gratitude for their goals as if they have already been achieved. This positive reinforcement is believed to create a mental state that attracts positive outcomes.

10, Alpha Sound technique

The Silva Method incorporates the use of the Alpha Sound Technique, where individuals mentally repeat the word "one" to help deepen their state of relaxation and access the alpha brainwave state.

11. Integrity and Daily Life

A key aspect of the Silva Method is the integration of its principles into daily life. Participants are encouraged to use the techniques regularly, not just during formal meditation sessions, to create a positive and proactive mindset.

The Silva Method operates on the premise that individuals can unlock their potential, overcome limitations, and create positive life changes by accessing the alpha state and engaging in specific mental exercises. The effectiveness of the method can vary from person to person, and individuals may choose to explore it to see how well it aligns with their personal goals and preferences.

The idea that everyone has the power to manifest positive changes is rooted in the belief that individuals possess the ability to influence their reality through their thoughts, beliefs, and actions. Here's an exploration of this concept:

Power of the Mind:

The foundation of the idea lies in recognising the power of the human mind. Thoughts are considered potent forces that shape perceptions, emotions, and behaviours. By harnessing the mind's creative potential, individuals can actively participate in shaping their experiences.

Law of Attraction:

Central to the concept is the law of attraction, which suggests that like attracts like. Positive thoughts and energy attract positive experiences, while negative thoughts can draw undesirable outcomes. This principle underscores the importance of maintaining an optimistic mindset.

Self-Fulfilling Prophecy:

The idea aligns with the concept of a self-fulfilling prophecy, where one's beliefs and expectations can influence behaviour in a way that makes those beliefs come true. By cultivating positive expectations and beliefs, individuals set the stage for positive outcomes.

Mind-Body Connection:

The mind-body connection plays a crucial role. Positive thoughts and emotions are believed to contribute to physical well-being, while negativity can impact health negatively. Recognising this connection empowers individuals to prioritise mental and emotional health for overall well-being.

Intention and Visualisation:

Individuals are encouraged to set clear intentions for what they want to manifest. Visualisation, a technique that involves vividly imagining desired outcomes, is often employed. This process engages the creative power of the mind to attract and manifest positive changes.

Belief in Personal Agency:

The concept emphasises an individual's agency and responsibility in creating their reality. It implies that regardless of external circumstances, individuals have the power to shape their responses and perspectives, influencing the outcomes they experience.

Resilience and Growth Mindset:

A resilient mindset and a growth mindset are inherent in the idea. Resilience allows individuals to bounce back from challenges, while a growth mindset fosters a belief in one's ability to learn, adapt, and overcome obstacles, contributing to positive change.

Positive Affirmations:

Positive affirmations, or consciously formulated positive statements, are often employed to reinforce positive beliefs. Regularly affirming positive qualities and desired outcomes helps shift thought patterns and encourages a more optimistic mindset.

Personal Development Practices:

Engaging in personal development practices, such as mindfulness, meditation, and gratitude, is encouraged. These practices contribute to emotional well-being, self-awareness, and a positive outlook on life.

Community and Support:

Acknowledging that individuals can benefit from supportive communities and networks is part of this idea. Positive environments and relationships can provide encouragement, inspiration, and a sense of collective empowerment.

Learning and Adaptation:

The concept recognises the importance of continuous learning and adaptation. Being open to new ideas, perspectives, and experiences contributes to personal growth and the manifestation of positive changes.

In essence, the idea that everyone has the power to manifest positive changes encourages individuals to take an active role in shaping their reality by cultivating a positive mindset, setting clear intentions, and aligning their thoughts and actions with the outcomes they wish to experience. It's a philosophy that emphasises personal empowerment and recognising the individual's creative capacity in influencing their life journey.

List of books for continued learning:

"The Secret" by Rhonda Byrne

"You Are a Badass: How to Stop Doubting Your Greatness and Start Living an Awesome Life" by Jen Sincero

"Think and Grow Rich" by Napoleon Hill

"The Power of Your Subconscious Mind" by Joseph Murphy

"Creative Visualisation: Use the Power of Your Imagination to Create What You Want in Your Life" by Shakti Gawain

"The Law of Attraction: The Basics of the Teachings of Abraham" by Esther Hicks and Jerry Hicks

"Manifest Now: A Process for Identifying and Reversing Limiting Beliefs" by Idil Ahmed

"E-Squared: Nine Do-It-Yourself Energy Experiments That Prove Your Thoughts Create Your Reality" by Pam Grout

"The Four Agreements: A Practical Guide to Personal Freedom" by Don Miguel Ruiz

"The Magic of Believing" by Claude M. Bristol

These books cover a range of manifestation principles, the law of attraction, mindset, and personal development, providing insights and practical guidance for those interested in manifesting positive changes in their lives.

Printed in Great Britain
by Amazon